Best Terrine Recipes

A perfect variety of vegetable, meat, cheese and dessert terrine dishes sure to impress family and guests

Imagine yourself presenting a beautiful dish such as this scrumptious Salmon Wrapped Cheese Terrine below to your co-workers, your spouse's employer, your family or friends. Needless to say, they will be asking you for the recipe! The decision is yours- will you give them your prized recipe or keep it a secret?

Do you need to bring dessert to a family gathering or work party? Imagine yourself walking in with this beautiful Tiramisu terrine dish below. This recipe and more awaits you in this book of terrine dishes.

Table of Contents

OTHER BOOKS BY DIANA LOERA

Summertime Sangria

Party Time Chicken Wing Recipes

Awesome Thanksgiving Leftovers Revive Guide

Best Venison Recipes

Meet Me at the County Fair – Fair Food Recipes

What is the Paleo Diet & Paleo Diet Recipe Sampler

12 Extra Special Summer Dessert Fondue Recipes

14 Extra Special Winter Holidays Fondue Recipes

USA Based Wholesale Directory 2014

Fast Start Guide to Flea Market Selling

I601A – Our Journey to Ciudad Juarez

Stop Hot Flashes Now

Please visit www.LoeraPublishing.com to view all titles and descriptions. Thank you.

WHAT IS A TYPICAL TERRINE DISH?

A terrine is a French loaf similar to a pâté, made with more coarsely chopped ingredients.

Terrines can be made of minced meat such as game or poultry, or seafood or vegetables. Dessert terrines can also be made from fruit.

The mixture is packed into a rectangular dish (sometimes also called a terrine) and cooked in a bain-marie.

Terrines are usually served cold or at room temperature.

Most meat terrines contain a large amount of fat as well as pork, although it is often not the main ingredient.

While terrines are common in the UK, they are not seen as often in the US, making them a unique and special dish to serve to family and guests.

If you are a bit nervous about making a terrine, I suggest starting with a cheese terrine or dessert terrine first.

Measurements for most recipes are based on UK standards. A measurement conversion chart is also included in this book for your convenience.

A List of Some Cooking Words Americans May Not be Familiar With

Sometimes the idea of making a recipe can be a bit overwhelming especially when words are used one may not be familiar with.

So that you do not have to stop reading and look up a word, I added in a few of the ones that seem to be the most unfamiliar to Americans. I think once you see the definitions you will realize the word is simply a different name for something you are familiar with.

After this list of words I've also included measurement conversion charts.

Bain Marie (also known as a water bath or double boiler), a type of heated bath, is a piece of equipment used in cooking to heat ingredients gently and gradually to fixed temperatures, or to keep materials warm over a period of time.

Fromage blanc (also known as maquée) is a fresh cheese originating from the north of France and the south of Belgium. The name means "white cheese" in French.

Streaky Bacon - Side bacon, or streaky bacon, comes from pork belly. It is very fatty with long layers of fat running parallel to the rind. This is the most common form of bacon in the United States

Film Wrap – Saran wrap or other cling wrap. Also sometimes called cling film.

Tin foil – aluminum foil

Terrine dishes are popular in the UK. Many of the recipes in this book use UK measurements. I've included the guide below to help readers quickly calculate the correct measurement needed.

The charts below use standard U.S. measures following U.S. Government guideline.

The charts offer equivalents for United States, metric, and Imperial (U.K.) measures.

All conversions are approximate and most have been rounded up or down to the nearest whole number.

Dry/Weight Measurements				
		Ounces	Pounds	Metric
1/16 teaspoon	a dash			
1/8 teaspoon or less	a pinch or 6 drops		.	.5 ml
1/4 teaspoon	15 drops			1 ml
1/2 teaspoon	30 drops			2 ml
1 teaspoon	1/3 tablespoon	1/6 ounce		5 ml
3 teaspoons	1 tablespoon	1/2 ounce		14 grams
1 tablespoon	3 teaspoons	1/2 ounce		14 grams
2 tablespoons	1/8 cup	1 ounce		28 grams
4 tablespoons	1/4 cup	2 ounces		56.7 grams
5 tablespoons plus 1 teaspoon	1/3 cup	2.6 ounces		75.6 grams
8 tablespoons	1/2 cup	4 ounces	1/4 pound	113 grams
10 tablespoons plus 2 teaspoons	2/3 cup	5.2 ounces		151 grams
12 tablespoons	3/4 cup	6 ounces	.375 pound	170 grams
16 tablespoons	1 cup	8 ounces	.500 pound or 1/2 pound	225 grams
32 tablespoons	2 cups	16 ounces	1 pound	454 grams
64 tablespoons	4 cups or 1	32	2 pounds	907

	quart	ounces		grams

Liquid or Volume Measurements

jigger or measure	1 1/2 or 1.5 fluid ounces		3 tablespoons	45 ml
1 cup	8 fluid ounces	1/2 pint	16 tablespoons	237 ml
2 cups	16 fluid ounces	1 pint	32 tablespoons	474 ml
4 cups	32 fluid ounces	1 quart	64 tablespoons	.946 ml
2 pints	32 fluid ounces	1 quart	4 cups	.964 liters
4 quarts	128 fluid ounces	1 gallon	16 cups	3.8 liters
8 quarts	256 fluid ounces or one peck	2 gallons	32 cups	7.5 liters
4 pecks	one bushel			
dash	less than 1/4 teaspoon			

Conversions For Ingredients Commonly Used In Baking

Ingredients	Ounces	Grams
1 cup all-purpose flour	5 ounces	142 grams
1 cup whole wheat flour	8 1/2 ounces	156 grams

1 cup granulated (white) sugar	7 ounces	198 grams
1 cup firmly-packed brown sugar (light or dark)	7 ounces	198 grams
1 cup powdered (confectioners') sugar	4 ounces	113 grams
1 cup cocoa powder	3 ounces	85 grams
Butter (salted or unsalted)		
4 tablespoons = 1/2 stick = 1/4 cup	2 ounces	57 grams
8 tablespoons = 1 stick = 1/2 cup	4 ounces	113 grams
16 tablespoons = 2 sticks = 1 cup	8 ounces	227 grams

Oven Temperatures			
Fahrenheit	**Celsius**	**Gas Mark (Imperial)**	**Description**
225 degrees F.	105 degrees C.	1/3	very cool
250 degrees F.	120 degrees C.	1/2	
275 degrees F.	130 degrees C.	1	cool
300 degrees F.	150 degrees	2	

	C.		
325 degrees F.	165 degrees C	3	very moderate
350 degrees F.	180 degrees C.	4	moderate
375 degrees F.	190 degrees C.	5	
400 degrees F.	200 degrees C.	6	moderately hot
425 degrees F.	220 degrees C.	7	hot
450 degrees F.	230 degrees C.	8	
475 degrees F.	245 degrees C.	9	very hot

In the first section of recipes, we will be using vegetables in our terrine dish.

Adding a vegetable based terrine dish to your meal planning provides family and friends with a unique addition to their meal.

As terrine dishes are made in advance, you can prepare these recipes beforehand, thus shortening your meal preparation time during the week.

BAKED CARROT TERRINE

PREPARATION TIME: 1 hour and 25 minutes

INGREDIENTS:

1 kg. washed carrots

6 eggs

500 g. evaporated milk

Salt

Pepper

Nutmeg

DIRECTIONS:

1. Peel and dice the carrots.

2. Cook carrots in one litre of salted water, drain and mash.

3. Mix the eggs with the evaporated milk and beat into the carrot purée.

4. Season with salt, pepper and nutmeg.

5. Fill the mould and bake in a bain-marie in the oven at 160º C for one hour.

6. Serve with lamb's lettuce and balsamic vinaigrette.

CARROT AND GINGER TERRINE

INGREDIENTS:

1 pound carrots, washed, trimmed, peeled and cut in 1/4-inch rounds

½ teaspoon turmeric

¼ cup water

1 ½ envelopes unflavored gelatin

¼ cup plus 2 tablespoons chicken broth

¼ cup Fromage blanc

2 ¼ teaspoons grated, peeled fresh ginger

Kosher salt to taste

Freshly ground black pepper

1 scallion, sliced thin

Spinach and coriander sauce (see recipe)

DIRECTIONS:

1.   Toss carrots with turmeric in a 13-by-9-by-2-inch oval dish. Cover tightly with microwave plastic wrap. Cook at 100 percent power in a high-power oven for 8 minutes. Prick plastic to release steam.

2.   Remove from oven and uncover. Transfer to a food processor and process until smooth.

3.   Place water in a glass 1-cup measure. Sprinkle gelatin over water. Let stand for 2 minutes. Stir. Cover with plastic wrap. Cook for 30 seconds. Prick plastic to release steam.

4.   Remove from oven and uncover. Pour into food processor with carrots. Add broth, Fromage blanc, ginger, salt and pepper. Process until completely smooth. Taste and adjust seasonings, if needed.

5.   Transfer mixture to a bowl and stir in scallion. Rinse a 2- to 3-cup mold with ice water. Do not dry. Scrape mixture into mold. Cover with plastic wrap and refrigerate for at least 4 hours.

6.   Unmold terrine and cut into slices. Spoon spinach and coriander sauce onto four plates. Place terrine slices over sauce and serve.

CARROT AND BACON TERRINE

PREPARATION TIME: 20 minutes

COOK TIME: 1 hour and 10 minutes

COOL TIME: 30 minutes

INGREDIENTS:

15g butter

1 small onion, peeled and finely chopped

400g carrots, washed, peeled, chopped and cooked until completely tender

3 eggs

175g soft cheese

175g spinach, wilted and squeezed dry

100g streaky bacon

Salt

Pepper

DIRECTIONS:

1. Heat the butter in a pan and sweat the onion until softened without colouring. Place in a food processor with the carrots, eggs, soft cheese and a little salt and pepper and blend until completely smooth.

2. Line a 500g loaf tin with baking parchment and spoon half the carrot mixture into the tin. Add the spinach in a single layer. Top with the remaining carrot mixture

3. Arrange the slices of streaky bacon on top and bake in the oven for about an hour. If the bacon gets too crisp, cover the tin with foil.

4. Remove from the oven, leave to cool a little in the tin then turn out onto a wire rack to cool completely.

VEGETABLES TERRINE

INGREDIENTS:

8 large beet greens or ruby Swiss chard

Salt and pepper

4 oz. cauliflower florets

4 oz. green peas

4 oz. carrots

4 oz. red pepper, seeded

1 ½ oz. grated Parmesan cheese

5 eggs

2 ¼ cup heavy cream

DIRECTIONS:

1. Bring a large pot of water to the boil. Salt it and blanch the beet greens, one minute. Remove the leaves and immediately rinse under ice cold water to set their colour. Gently lay on tea towels, and pat dry with another tea towel. They should not have any water on them for the next step.

2. Line a buttered terrine mould with a piece of parchment. Neatly lay in the beet leaves to cover the bottom and sides completely. They should dangle over the sides a bit so that they can be folded over the completed terrine later.

3. Cook the cauliflower, peas, and carrots, one at a time in the same pot of boiling salted water, until very tender. Remove them and immediately rinse in ice-cold water to preserve their colour. Drain well. Roast the pepper until very soft, peel, seed, and cut into pieces.

4. This terrine has five layers, so work one vegetable at a time. First put the cauliflower in the blender with one egg and 1/4 cup/60 ml cream. Pulse to a smooth purée. Pour into a small bowl and set aside. Rinse the blender and proceed with the remaining vegetables in the same manner, pouring their purées off into bowls and setting aside. Put the final egg and 1/4 cup/60 ml cream in the blender with the Parmesan cheese and purée to blend. Season each mixture with salt and pepper to taste.

5. If you pour one mixture in on top of the other into the terrine, they will run together, so spoon them in instead. Start with the carrot, spooning it into the terrine and smoothing it out to the edges. Next, spoon over the cauliflower, followed by the peas. Spoon the Parmesan mixture over evenly, and end with the red pepper. If one leaks through to another layer, fear not: some think it is even more beautiful that way and in any case it will taste delicious. Fold the overhanging beet leaves over top to cover. Bake in a water bath at 350°F/180°C until set, a good hour.

6. Remove the terrine from the bath. Let it cool completely on a wire rack, and, if possible, chill in the refrigerator overnight so it sets well. At least half an hour before serving, turn the terrine out onto a cutting board or platter for serving in slices.

CAULIFLOWER TERRINE

PREPARATION TIME: 55 minutes

COOK TIME: 30 minutes

INGREDIENTS:

250 g cauliflower, steamed

4 tsp grated ginger

2 limes, zest only

1/2 tsp salt

150 ml coconut cream

30 g ground almonds

250 g carrots, peeled and cooked

1/2 tsp sugar, (optional)

FOR THE DRESSING:

4 tsp grated ginger

2 tbsp. sweet chili sauce

2 tbsp. chopped fresh mint

40 g salted peanuts, very finely ground

3-4 tbsp. lime juice

DIRECTIONS:

1. Preheat the oven to 190C/Gas 5.

2. Put the steamed cauliflower together with 2 teaspoons grated ginger, zest of 1 lime, ¼ teaspoon salt and 5 tablespoons of the coconut cream into a food processor and process for about 20-30 seconds. Turn into a bowl and mix in 3 tablespoons of the ground almonds.

3. Put the steamed carrots with 2 teaspoons grated ginger, zest of 1 lime, ¼ tsp salt, and the remaining coconut cream into a food processor and process for about 20-30 seconds. If the carrots are not very sweet, add ½ tsp caster sugar. Turn out into a separate bowl and mix in the remaining 2 ½ tablespoons of ground almonds.

4. Grease a 450g non-stick loaf tin and line with baking parchment. Divide both vegetable mixtures into two, and layer them in the prepared loaf time starting with the carrot mixture. (It is easier to put each layer on top of the other by blobbing the mixture all over the previous layer and then spreading it gently over, rather than putting all the mixture in at once.)

5. Bake the terrine in the preheated oven for about 30 minutes until well set. Half way through, cover the top with tin foil if it starts to brown. Let it cool in the tin for about 10 minutes before turning out and cooling completely. Chill well in the fridge before serving.

6. To make the dressing: Mix all of the dressing ingredient above together. The dressing should be quite thick rather than runny. I like to let the dressing sit 30-60 minutes if possible so the ingredients mesh.

7. Slice the terrine and serve with the dressing on the side.

ASPARAGUS TERRINE

PREPARATION TIME: 35 minutes

COOK TIME: 2 hours

INGREDIENTS:

2 teaspoons unflavored powdered gelatin

2 tablespoons cold water

8 ounces quark or farmers cheese, room temperature

8 ounces cream cheese, room temperature

3 to 5 good quality, jarred anchovies in olive oil, drained

7 whole, fresh chives

1/2 teaspoon freshly ground black pepper

1/4 cup roughly chopped flat-leaf parsley

1 recipe Steamed Asparagus, cooled, recipe follows

Toasted French bread slices, for serving

Special equipment: Spritz bottle filled with water or use the sprayer attachment on your sink (just use a light touch)

Steamed Asparagus:

1/4 cup water

1 pound fresh asparagus, 1 to 1 1/2 inches cut off the bottom

1/2 teaspoon kosher salt

DIRECTIONS:

1. Spritz a 9 by 5-inch loaf pan with water and line it with plastic wrap, leaving enough excess to fold over the top when filled.

2. Combine the gelatin and water in a 1-quart saucepan and set aside to bloom for 5 minutes.

3. Put the quark, cream cheese, anchovies, chives, and black pepper in the bowl of a food processor and process for 1 minute. Stop and scrape down the sides of the bowl.

4. Put the bloomed gelatin over low heat until melted, about 1 minute. Remove from the heat. With the food processor running, slowly pour the melted gelatin into the cheese mixture and process for 30 seconds.

5. Sprinkle the parsley evenly across the bottom of the prepared loaf pan. Pour 1/4 of the cheese mixture over the parsley. Top with 1/3 of the asparagus in a single layer, alternating direction of tips. Repeat with remaining cheese mixture and asparagus, ending with the cheese mixture. Fold the excess plastic wrap over the filling. Set a second loaf pan on top of the plastic wrap and press down to compact. Refrigerate until firm, about 2 hours.

6. Serve chilled, cut into 1-inch slices, along with crackers or toasted French bread slices.

CHICKEN SAUSAGE TERRINE

3 lbs. cooked chicken

1 lb. (raw) pork sausage meat

½ lb. boiled sliced ham

2 cloves (10gm) finely chopped garlic

2 beaten eggs

1 teaspoon tarragon

1 tablespoon chopped parsley

¼ cup (4 tbsp.) brandy

½ teaspoon salt

1 ground black pepper

½ cup (8 tbsp.) softened butter

½ lbs. bacon slices

DIRECTIONS:

1. Discard the skin and bone and cut the chicken into small pieces.

2. Put chopped chicken to one side.

3. Stir together all remaining ingredients except the bacon.

4. Line a glass or ceramic casserole with half the bacon slices.

5. Cover with one-third of the sausage mixture and top with half the chicken.

6. Continue forming layers, top with the sausage mixture, and cover with the remaining bacon.

7. Cook in the microwave oven on roast setting for 25 minutes.

8. Rotate the dish one quarter of a turn after 15 minutes.

9. Allow the terrine to cool.

10. Place it in the refrigerator and weight it with 3 1lb (16oz) canned goods so it can be sliced without crumbling.

11. Chill 12 hours before serving.

12: Remove from refrigerator, remove canned goods and slice terrine.

CHICKEN LIVER TERRINE

INGREDIENTS:

1/4 cup sugar

2 tablespoons water

10 medium shallots, coarsely chopped

5 tablespoons Cognac

3 sticks (3/4 pound) plus 4 tablespoons unsalted butter, at cool room temperature, cut into tablespoons

2 pounds chicken livers, cleaned

Kosher salt and freshly ground pepper

Cornichons and toasted sourdough bread, for serving

DIRECTIONS:

1. In a medium saucepan, combine the sugar with the water and simmer over moderate heat, without stirring, until an amber caramel forms, about 8 minutes. Add the shallots and stir well, then add the Cognac. Cover and simmer over low heat, stirring occasionally, until the caramel dissolves and the shallots are soft, about 10 minutes. Spread the mixture in a large dish and refrigerate for 20 minutes.

2. In a large skillet, melt the 4 tablespoons of butter. Add the chicken livers and season with salt and pepper. Cook over high heat until firm on both sides and deep pink in the center, about 3 minutes per side. Transfer the livers and their juices to a shallow dish and let cool to room temperature. Refrigerate the livers for 20 minutes.

3. In a food processor, combine the livers with the shallot mixture and process until pureed. With the machine on, gradually add the remaining 3 sticks of butter until thoroughly incorporated. Strain the puree through a fine sieve set over a large bowl. Season with salt and pepper.

4. Line a 4-cup terrine or loaf pan with sheets of plastic wrap, leaving a 3-inch overhang all around. Scrape the puree into the terrine and cover tightly with the overhanging plastic wrap. Refrigerate until very firm, at least overnight and for up to 5 days. Unwrap the terrine and turn it out on a platter. Serve chilled, with cornichons and sourdough toasts.

LAYERED CHEESE TERRINE

PREPARATION TIME: 40 minutes

TOTAL TIME: 100 minutes

INGREDIENTS:

2 cup (500 ml) shredded Canadian Gouda

¼ cup (50 ml) chopped parsley

4 tsp (20 ml) milk

½ tsp (2.5 ml) salt

1 tub (250 g) Canadian Cream Cheese with roasted garlic

2 Tbsp. (30 ml) chopped green onions

Black pepper, to taste

2 cup (500 ml) shredded Canadian Cheddar

½ tubs (125 g) package plain Canadian Cream Cheese, cubed

1 Tbsp. (15 ml) chopped pickled hot red peppers or half a sweet pepper, chopped

DIRECTIONS:

1. In a food processor bowl fitted with metal blade, combine Gouda, chopped parsley, milk and salt. Process until smooth.

2. Line a 6-cup (1.5-litre) glass dish or aluminum loaf pan with foil. Spread mixture in dish or pan.

3. Cream together Cream Cheese with roasted garlic, chopped green onions and black pepper. Spread mixture over Gouda layer.

4. In clean bowl of food processor, combine Cheddar and plain Cream Cheese and process until smooth. Stir in chopped peppers. Spread mixture over roasted garlic Cream Cheese layer.

5. Cover and chill for 1 hour or up to 4 days.

6. Serve with an assortment of crackers

CHEESE TERRINE WRAPPED WITH SMOKE SALMON

INGREDIENTS:

400 g (13oz) smoked salmon slices

200 g (7 oz.) cream cheese

100 ml (3½ fl oz.) Cream

1 lemon, juice and grated rind

1 tbsp. capers, chopped

1 tbsp. tarragon

Pepper, to season

DIRECTIONS:

1. Place the cream cheese into a food processor and add the cream, lemon juice and rind, herbs and capers, blitz for 1-2 minutes until all the ingredients are combined. Remove contents to a glass bowl and season with some pepper.

2. In the meantime, double line a loaf tin with Saran Wrap, allowing an overhang of at least 5cm all-round.

3. Place a layer of smoked salmon on the base of the lined loaf tin, then using a spatula, spread one third of the mixture over the salmon. Repeat the layers ensuring you finish with a layer of smoked salmon.

4. Wrap the Saran Wrap over the loaf tin and place a plate on top. Place in the fridge for 24 hours. Serve with bread and/or crackers.

SALMON AND AVOCADO TERRINE

INGREDIENTS:

1 1/4 pounds salmon fillet, cut into 1/2inch cubes

1 teaspoon salt

1 teaspoon freshly ground black pepper

3 cups fish stock or clam juice

1 tablespoon unsalted butter

3 shallots, thinly sliced

1/2 cup thinly sliced mushrooms

1 cup brandy

2 tablespoons unflavored gelatin

2 dashes of Tabasco

1 1/2 cups cold heavy cream

4 ounces thinly sliced smoked salmon, cut into 5 by 1 1/2inch strips across the grain

1 ripe avocado, peeled, pitted, and thinly sliced

DIRECTIONS:

1. To make the mousse, preheat the oven to 350 degrees. Place the fresh salmon in a single layer in a medium ovenproof skillet and sprinkle with salt and pepper. Bring the fish stock to a boil and pour it over the salmon. Over medium high heat, bring the stock to a simmer. Place a buttered sheet of parchment paper over the skillet and transfer it to the oven. Cook for 2 minutes, until the salmon is not quite done. Strain, reserving the salmon and stock in separate bowls.

2. In a medium saucepan, heat the butter over medium low heat. Add the shallots and the mushrooms and cook for about 3 minutes, or until almost tender. Add the brandy and flame it with a match, standing well away from the pan. Cook over high heat until reduced by half, then add the reserved stock and again reduce by half. Remove from the heat and sprinkle the gelatin over the top. Stir until the gelatin has dissolved, then strain into a food processor and discard the solids. Add the cooked salmon and the Tabasco to the food processor and puree the mixture until smooth. Whip the cream to soft peaks and reserve in the refrigerator. Transfer the salmon mixture to a metal bowl set inside a larger bowl filled with ice water. Stir until the mixture has cooled to room temperature, but not colder. Stir in 1/4 of the whipped cream to loosen the mixture, then fold in the remaining whipped cream gently.

3. Stop folding as soon as the last trace of white disappears. Pour 1/2 of the mixture into a 10 by 5 by 3inch glass loaf pan and, using half of the smoked salmon, gently lay a layer of smoked salmon over the top, laying the strips crosswise. Fit the avocado slices together into an even layer, taking care not to press down too hard or the mousse underneath will shift. Lay the remaining smoked salmon over the top of the avocado and then scoop the remaining salmon mousse into the pan. Spread the mousse into an even layer and cover with plastic wrap. Chill for at least 6 hours and up to 2 days before serving. To serve, run a thin knife along the inside edge of the pan. Dip the bottom of the pan in hot water for a few seconds and invert onto a rectangular serving platter. Cut the mousse into 3/4inch slices with a very sharp knife transfer carefully to serving plates. Pass the watercress mayonnaise on the side.

TERRINE WITH THREE CHEESES

INGREDIENTS:

1x100 g buffalo mozzarella, drained

4 ox (110 g) gorgonzola picante

1.250 g tub ricotta

5 leaves gelatin (or 1x11 g sachet powdered gelatin or a vegetarian alternative)

3 fl oz. (75 ml) mayonnaise

1 dessert spoon lemon juice

5 fl oz. (150 ml) double cream

2 spring onions, finely chopped

1 level teaspoon chopped fresh dill

1 level dessertspoon snipped fresh chives

Salt and freshly milled black pepper

DIRECTIONS:

1. Start off by dealing with the gelatin. If you are using leaves, add them to plenty of cold water and soak for 4 minutes (longer wouldn't hurt). If you are using powder, sprinkle it into a cup or basin containing 2-3 tablespoons of water. Stir, and when the gelatin has soaked up the liquid, place the bowl or cup in a pan of barely simmering water and leave until the gelatin has dissolved completely and turned transparent. To test this, dip a teaspoon in, turn it over and you'll soon see if there are any undissolved granules.

2. Meanwhile, dice the Mozzarella and Gorgonzola into ¼ inch (5 mm) pieces and combine. Then blend the ricotta, mayonnaise and lemon juice together until absolutely smooth. Next whip up the double cream until it has thickened to the floppy stage; it should not be too thick.

3. Remove the gelatin leaves from the water, squeeze them out and put them in a medium saucepan. Melt over a gentle heat – this will only take about 30 seconds. Once the gelatin has melted, remove the pan from the heat then add the ricotta. Stir the mixture really well to distribute the gelatin evenly, then add the diced Mozzarella and Gorgonzola, spring onions, herbs and a good seasoning of salt and freshly milled black pepper. (If using powdered gelatin, just add the ricotta to the dissolved gelatin and proceed as above.)

4. Finally, fold in the cream and turn the whole lot into the prepared tin. This should be done speedily or else it will begin to set. Cover with cling film and chill in the fridge for several hours till firmly set.

5. To turn out the terrine, carefully slide a palette knife around the edge of the tin, invert on to a serving plate and give the base a sharp tap. Serve the terrine in slices.

BLUE CHEESE AND SPICED WALNUT TERRINE

INGREDIENTS:

1/2 teaspoon salt

1/2 teaspoon ground cumin

1/4 teaspoon ground cardamom

1/4 teaspoon ground black pepper

1 tablespoon olive oil

1 cup walnuts

3 tablespoons sugar

16 ounces blue cheese, crumbled

2 1/2 ounces soft fresh goat cheese (such as Montrachet)

2 1/2 ounces cream cheese, room temperature

1/4 cup (1/2 stick) butter, room temperature

1/2 cup chopped green onions

2 tablespoons brandy

2 tablespoons chopped fresh parsley

1 tablespoon chopped chives

Red leaf lettuce

DIRECTIONS:

1. Mix salt, cumin, cardamom and pepper in medium bowl. Heat oil in heavy medium skillet over medium heat. Add walnuts and sauté until light brown, about 5 minutes. Sprinkle sugar over nuts and sauté until sugar melts and turns pale amber, about 4 minutes. Transfer nut mixture to bowl with spices; toss to coat well. Let cool. Coarsely chop nuts.

2. Lightly oil 8 1/2 x 2 1/2-inch loaf pan. Line pan with plastic wrap so that plastic extends over edges. Combine 12 ounces blue cheese, goat cheese, cream cheese and butter in processor and blend until smooth. Transfer mixture to large bowl. Stir in green onions and brandy. Mix parsley and chives in small bowl.

3. Spoon 1/3 of cheese mixture into bottom of lined pan, spreading evenly. Sprinkle 1/3 of remaining crumbled blue cheese evenly over cheese mixture. Sprinkle 1/3 of nuts over blue cheese. Sprinkle with 1 tablespoon of herb mixture. Repeat layering. Spread remaining cheese mixture evenly over top. Fold plastic over cheese to cover. Refrigerate overnight. Cover remaining blue cheese and herbs separately and refrigerate. Store remaining nuts at room temperature.

4. Line platter with lettuce leaves. Unfold plastic from cheese. Carefully invert mold onto platter; remove pan and plastic. Sprinkle terrine with remaining blue cheese, nuts and herbs.

BLUE CHEESE AND FRUIT TERRINE

PREPARATION TIME: 25 minutes

TOTAL TIME: 1 hour and 30 minutes

INGREDIENTS:

10 oz. (283 g) blue cheese, crumbled

1 pkg (5 oz./142 g) soft goat cheese, crumbled

1/3 cup (75 mL) finely chopped dried apricots

1/4 cup (60 mL) finely chopped dried pears

1/4 cup (60 mL) finely chopped prunes

2 tbsp. (30 mL) liquid honey

4 tsp (18 mL) brandy

3/4 tsp (4 mL) chopped fresh thyme

1 pinch pepper

1/2 cup (125 mL) walnut halves

1/2 cup (125 mL) almonds

DIRECTIONS:

1. Line 8- x 4-inch (1.5 L) loaf pan with plastic wrap, leaving enough overhang to cover top. Set aside.

2. In large bowl, combine blue cheese, goat cheese, apricots, pears and prunes. Drizzle with 4 tsp of the honey and the brandy; sprinkle with thyme and pepper. Gently toss to combine.

3. Scrape into prepared pan; fold plastic wrap overhang over top to cover completely. Press down gently to compact. Refrigerate for 1 hour. (Make-ahead: Refrigerate for up to 2 days.)

4. Meanwhile, in skillet, toast walnuts and almonds over medium-low heat, shaking pan often, until fragrant, about 5 minutes. Let cool.

5. Turn out terrine onto cutting board and peel off plastic wrap; arrange on plate. Surround with nuts; drizzle with remaining honey.

BEET AND GOAT CHEESE TERRINE

INGREDIENTS:

About 12 beet roots, in as many different colours as you can find.

Soft goat cheese, about 500 grams / 1 pound

Salt and Pepper

Olive oil

2 bread tins

Basil leaves, pistachios and any kind of edible flower for garnish

Maldon Salt for finishing.

Sharp knife

DIRECTIONS:

1. Cook the beets in boiling water until soft, about 30 minutes.

2. Peel and let cool.

3. Slice very thinly.

4. Line one of the bread tins with plastic wrap leaving some overhang to fold over once the terrine is completed.

5. Start layering the beets and goat cheese, as if you were making a lasagna, seasoning with salt and pepper and a small drizzle of olive oil between layers.

6. Start with the lighter coloured beets first, i.e. golden beets, followed by a layer of goat cheese, followed by more golden beets, until they are finished.

7. Then repeat with the red beets and goat cheese, making sure that the last layer is beets.

8. Your finished terrine may not reach the top of the dish but that is okay.

9. Once you have finished the layering, fold the plastic over to seal.

10. Place a weight on the terrine so it compresses. 3 16 oz. canned goods work well.

11. Place in the refrigerator for at least 8 hours, or overnight.

12. When you are ready to serve, pull the terrine out of the tin on to a board. Unwrap the terrine and carefully slice (with that very sharp knife), making each slice about 1/2 an inch or 15mm thick.

13. Trim the edges for a nice presentation.

14. Place the slices on a long platter and decorate with basil leaves. You can also use decorative flowers or leaves.

15. Optional- lightly sprinkle with sea salt.

16. Serve with crusty bread and a salad.

BLUE CHEESE TERRINE WITH TOMATO-BASIL VINAIGRETTE

INGREDIENTS:

2 red bell peppers, cut in half

2 yellow bell peppers, cut in half

6 ounces blue cheese, crumbled

2 (8-ounce) packages cream cheese, softened

Tomato-Basil Vinaigrette (found in salad dressing aisle)

Mixed salad greens

DIRECTIONS:

1.   Place bell pepper halves, cut sides down, on an aluminum foil-lined baking sheet.

2.   Broil 5 inches from heat 8 to 10 minutes or until bell peppers look blistered.

3.   Place bell peppers in a heavy-duty zip-top plastic bag; seal and let stand 10 minutes to loosen skins. Peel peppers; remove and discard seeds. Pat dry with paper towels.

4.   Beat cheeses at medium speed with an electric mixer until smooth.

5.   Spread half of cheese mixture in a plastic wrap-lined 8- x 4-inch loaf pan. Top with 4 pepper halves. Spread remaining cheese mixture over peppers; top with remaining pepper halves. Chill 8 hours.

6.   Unmold onto a serving dish, and drizzle with Tomato-Basil Vinaigrette. Serve on mixed greens.

GOAT CHEESE AND HERB TERRINE

INGREDIENTS:

3 or 4 young zucchini

3 or 4 young carrots

220 g fresh goat cheese

180 g faisselle (substitute half thick yogurt and half cottage cheese)

3 eggs

5 sprigs of fresh flat-leaf parsley

10 leaves of fresh basil

Salt

Pepper

DIRECTIONS:

1. Put the faisselle in a colander to drain for a few hours beforehand. Rinse the parsley and basil, pat dry with a paper towel, and chop the leaves. Wash and dry the vegetables, peel the carrots.

2. Trim the ends, and cut all veggies in little sticks, not too thin. Steam them for ten minutes, until cooked al dente.

3. Preheat the oven to 180°C (360°F). Grease a terrine dish (or loaf pan), and line the bottom with baking parchment.

4. In a medium mixing-bowl, combine the goat cheese, the faisselle, and the eggs, and beat with a fork until blended. Season with salt and pepper, and add in the parsley and basil.

5. Pour a first layer of cheese mixture in the terrine, even it out with a spatula. Lay sticks of vegetables on top in a parallel pattern, alternating the colors. Pour another layer of cheese, then more vegetables. Repeat with the rest of the ingredients, ending with a layer of vegetables.

6. The number of layers and sticks per layer will depend on the size of your dish but you do not want to over crowd.

7. Put the terrine dish in a wider baking dish, and pour a half-inch of water in the baking dish : this is called "bain-marie", a technique which will ensure a more even cooking, and will prevent the batter from boiling. Put this into the oven to bake for 50 minutes.

8. Let cool to room temperature, then let rest in the refrigerator for at least 8 hours. When ready to serve, run a knife around the edges to loosen the terrine, flip onto a plate, remove the layer of parchment paper from the bottom, then flip again onto a serving dish. Use a serrated knife and proceed with caution to cut slices or half-slices. Serve with good crusty bread.

DESSERT TERRINES

STRAWBERRY TERRINE

PREPARATION TIME: 10 minutes

SETTING TIME: 165 minutes

TOTAL TIME: 175 minutes

INGREDIENTS:

75g / 3 oz. caster / fine sugar

450ml/ 2 cups blueberry juice drink

150ml / 2/3 cup cold water

8 gelatin leaves

350g / 12 oz. Strawberries

2 x 150g / 5 oz. strawberry and cream yogurt

Fresh mint leaves

DIRECTIONS:

1. Chill a 900g / 2 lb. loaf tin in the freezer.

2. Meanwhile, put the caster sugar and blueberry juice drink into a pan and heat gently, stirring occasionally. Once the sugar has dissolved, boil the rapidly for 1 min. Leave to cool slightly.

3. Place the cold water into a small bowl, break the gelatin leaves in to a few large pieces and place into the water making sure they are covered with the water. Leave to soak for 2-3 minutes.

4. Take the gelatin from the water, squeeze gently then stir into the warm (but not hot) Add juice and stir until the gelatin has dissolved.

5. Hull and quarter the strawberries then scatter into the chilled loaf tin. Pour over half the gelatin mix and freeze for 45 minutes or until set.

6. Mix the remaining juice mixture with the pots of strawberries and cream yogurt and spoon over the set jelly. Chill in the fridge for at least 2 hrs. or until set.

7. To serve, fill a small roasting tin with warm water and dip the loaf tin into the water for 30-40 seconds. Place a plate over the top of the jelly, quickly turn the plate and tin over and lift the tin off.

Decorate the terrine with the remaining British hulled and quartered strawberries, and fresh mint leaves.

Note:

Gelatin comes in either leaves, powder or granules. Leaf gelatin is the more preferred setting agent in making a jelly than powdered as it gives a very clear, clean, tasteless set.

DARK CHOCOLATE AND COFFEE TERRINE

INGREDIENTS:

Valrhona Chocolate Terrine:

250g unsalted butter, chopped

250g caster sugar

250g Valrhona Guanaja chocolate, chopped

5 eggs

1 tablespoon flour

Coffee Bean Anglaise:

500ml cream

5 egg yolks

100g sugar

30ml espresso

1 teaspoon finely ground fresh coffee beans

To serve:

Icing sugar for dusting

Whipped cream

1 teaspoon freeze-dried plum powder

DIRECTIONS:

Valrhona Chocolate Terrine

1. Preheat the oven to 180°C. Place the butter in a deep bowl. Pour the sugar over the butter, then place the chocolate on top (this is so the butter and sugar dissolve and line the bowl, preventing the chocolate from sticking). Place the bowl over a saucepan of barely simmering water, ensuring the bowl doesn't touch the water, until the chocolate has melted, then remove from the heat. Transfer the mixture to an electric mixer with the whisk attachment fitted.

2. In a separate bowl, whisk the eggs with the flour. With the mixer running, pour the egg mixture into the chocolate and continue to whisk until the mixture becomes smooth and shiny.

3. Line a terrine or loaf tin with baking paper and pour in the chocolate mixture. Cover with a lid or tinfoil and place in a deep roasting dish. Pour in water to halfway up the sides of the terrine or tin and place in the oven for 1 hour, until it is slightly glossy in the center. Refrigerate overnight to set.

Coffee Bean Anglaise

1. In a saucepan, bring the cream to the boil, then set aside. Beat the egg yolks and sugar together until pale. Slowly add the cream to the sugar and yolk mixture while whisking continuously. Return to a moderate heat and cook, stirring continuously, until the custard coats the back of a wooden spoon. Remove from the heat and add the espresso and coffee beans. Cool in the refrigerator until ready to serve.

COFFEE TERRINE

PREPARATION TIME: 20 minutes

TOTAL TIME: 4 hours and 20 minutes

INGREDIENTS:

1 cup(s) heavy cream

1 container (6-ounce) container coffee yogurt

1/4 cup sugar

1/4 cup freshly brewed coffee, chilled

1 teaspoon pure vanilla extract

1 (10.75-ounce) frozen pound cake, such as Sara Lee, cut into 12 slices

1/2 cup semi -sweet chocolate chips, roughly chopped

2 tablespoons coffee beans, roughly chopped

DIRECTIONS:

1. Line a 4 1/2- by 8 1/2-inch loaf pan with parchment, leaving a 3-inch overhang on the long sides. Using an electric mixer on high, beat heavy cream, coffee yogurt, sugar, freshly brewed coffee, and vanilla extract in a large bowl until very thick, about 2 to 3 minutes.

2. Spread a quarter of the coffee mixture in the bottom of the loaf pan. Top with 4 slices of cake. Repeat twice with the remaining coffee mixture and cake. Spread the remaining coffee mixture over the top.

3. Sprinkle with chocolate chips and coffee beans. Freeze until set, at least 4 hours.

4. Once set, cover with plastic wrap and freeze for up to 1 week. To serve, let the terrine sit at room temperature for 5 minutes and run a knife around the edges, then use the overhangs to transfer the terrine to a platter.

TIRAMISU TERRINE

INGREDIENTS:

1 (8 oz.) container mascarpone cheese

½ cup confectioner's sugar

1 cup very strong coffee (note- you'll use 3 tablespoons of it then the remainder)

1/2 gallon your favorite vanilla ice cream

1 box ladyfingers

DIRECTIONS:

1 Mix together the mascarpone cheese, sugar and 3 tablespoons of the coffee.

2 Line a loaf pan with plastic wrap. Dunk ½ of the ladyfingers, one by one, in the strong coffee, and line the outside of the pan. Do the bottom as well – which will end up being the top.

3 Pour some of the mascarpone mixture on the bottom, then layer with ice cream, some dunked ladyfingers, over and over until you reach the top. Cover with plastic wrap and freeze.

4 Once ready to serve, pull it out by the lined plastic wrap and invert onto a plate. Slice as you would a cake.

FROZEN MOCHA TOFFEE CRUNCH TERRINE

INGREDIENTS:

19 chocolate wafer cookies

11 ounces mascarpone or cream cheese

1/2 cup sugar

1 tablespoon vanilla extract

1 1/4 cups heavy cream

1/2 cup toffee bits

1/3 cup semisweet chocolate chips, melted and cooled

1 tablespoon unsweetened cocoa powder

2 tablespoons instant-coffee granules

DIRECTIONS:

1. Line a 9-by-5-inch loaf pan with 2 sheets of plastic wrap, with long sides overhanging by about 3 inches. Arrange 3 wafers, flat side up, in a row in the bottom of the pan.

2. In a large bowl, beat mascarpone and sugar until light and fluffy. Stir in vanilla. In another bowl, beat cream until it holds soft peaks. In three additions, fold the whipped cream into the sweetened mascarpone with a rubber spatula.

3. In a bowl, mix 1 1/3 cups mascarpone mixture with toffee bits. In a separate bowl, mix another 1 1/3 cups mascarpone mixture with chocolate and cocoa powder. Dissolve the coffee in 1 teaspoon hot water; stir into the remaining mascarpone mixture.

4. Spread coffee mixture in prepared pan. Cover with 8 wafers, overlapping if necessary. Spoon chocolate mixture into pan; cover with 8 wafers. Spoon toffee mixture into pan.

5. Wrap pan with overhanging plastic; freeze at least 4 hours and up to 2 weeks. To serve, invert onto a serving platter. Remove plastic. Let terrine sit 5 minutes, then cut into slices.

Thank you for reading Best Terrine Recipes.

If you are interested in creating nougat (torrone) candies for the holidays or anytime, you may be interested in my latest book Best Christmas Nougat Recipes.

Readers will find nougat candy recipes sure to delight family and friends such as one for Christmas Nougat and Torrone.   You'll find this book and others on Amazon, Kindle and www.LoeraPublishing.com

Thank you for purchasing this book.   I hope you enjoy the recipes as much as I do.

If you are interested in finding different recipes, I hope you'll visit www.LoeraPublishing.com as you'll find numerous other books by me including recipes, wholesale sources and health related topics.

Summertime Sangria

Party Time Chicken Wing Recipes

Awesome Thanksgiving Leftovers Revive Guide

Best Venison Recipes

Meet Me at the County Fair – Fair Food Recipes

What is the Paleo Diet & Paleo Diet Recipe Sampler

12 Extra Special Summer Dessert Fondue Recipes

14 Extra Special Winter Holidays Fondue Recipes

USA Based Wholesale Directory 2014

Fast Start Guide to Flea Market Selling

I601A – Our Journey to Ciudad Juarez

Stop Hot Flashes Now

Please visit www.LoeraPublishing.com to view all titles and descriptions. Thank you.

Printed in Great Britain
by Amazon

36102118R00034